The Multifamily Real Estate Booklet

How to Share the Benefits of Multifamily Investing

to Create Financial Independence

Jake & Gino

The Multifamily Real Estate Booklet

How to Share the Benefits of Multifamily Investing
to Create Financial Independence

Join the Jake & Gino Facebook Community.

➤ **Share** with us your testimonials, comments, and more.

➤ **For updates** and news at Jake & Gino

➤ **Like our page** at https://www.facebook.com/JakeandGino

Also

To order additional copies, including quantity discounts, see below:

SPECIAL QUANTITY PRICING
Retail $12

1-9	$9
10-14	$6.50
25-99	$5
100+	$3.50

Plus shipping. Based on location and weight.

To Order, please:
E-mail: Hello@jakeandgino.com | Call: (865) 320-0662
www.jakeandgino.com/books

"Let your job pay for your apartments, and let your apartments pay for your lifestyle."

– Gino Barbaro

TABLE OF CONTENTS

PREFACE

This book is for you—all the Jake & Gino members out there grinding and growing your multifamily businesses.

I received the "epiphany" to write this book during a coaching call with Ryan and Mina, two MIH (Make It Happen) members who were excited to discuss multifamily investing with their inner circle of friends and family. They just weren't sure how to start the conversations.

Even if you've mastered the content, it's not always easy to convey your enthusiasm and expertise to someone who may have never heard of multifamily real estate. And once you introduce this amazing investing vehicle to friends and family, how do you continue to present the benefits so they can understand without being overwhelmed?

Here's the good news: You don't need your own podcast, blog, or YouTube channel to share the opportunity. You simply need a clear, concise message that outlines the benefits of multifamily investing and the ability to connect with others on a personal level.

In *The Multifamily Real Estate Booklet*, I will encourage you to create your own personal story—your own WHY for multifamily investing. You can then follow the framework laid out in this booklet to educate your potential investors. (I will use friends and family interchangeably with investors.) Once you read this book, you'll be equipped with everything you need to navigate these conversations confidently.

I made a commitment to our community to continue to educate and inspire a new generation of multifamily entrepreneurs. I challenge you to take the information I share and implement it in your business, so that you can provide an opportunity that most friends and family members will never have.

—Gino

INTRODUCTION

In *The Multifamily Real Estate Booklet: How to Offer the Opportunity to Friends & Family,* we want to simplify the process of raising capital from potential investors.

As you present the multifamily investing opportunity to your friends and family, they will inevitably have three questions:

1. *Can you help me?*

2. *Can I trust you?*

3. *Do you care about me?*

Your investors need to give an emphatic YES to each of those questions. *Can you help me?* **Yes, you can!** *Can I trust you?* **Yes, I can!** *Do you care about me?* **Yes to that, too!**

Once your investors feel confident about your ability to help them and feel they can trust you, you are well on your way to raising all the capital you need for all of your deals.

In case you don't know us, Jake and I own a vertically integrated real estate company that features a property management, investment, education, and capital company. We've grown our portfolio to over $100,000,000 in assets under management, raised over $10,000,000 in capital for our deals, and created the Jake & Gino community to help others achieve financial freedom and become the next multifamily entrepreneurs.

We wrote this booklet for the Jake & Gino community member looking to grow their multifamily business by raising capital for their acquisitions. As you progress through the booklet, you will begin to create your own personal framework to offer the opportunity to your investors. Once you are finished reading, you will be able to:

- Create your own story to build trust with your investors.

- Describe the asset multifamily in simple terms for your investors.

- Teach investors how multifamily works.

- Explain to investors how they get paid.

- Illustrate how multifamily vastly outperforms most other asset classes.

You will find Jake & Gino "isms" sprinkled throughout the booklet. Feel free to use these in your conversations with investors. They've proven to work for us!

Here's the truth: If you don't share with friends and family, they may never know how to participate in one of the best wealth creators in America—multifamily real estate. So, take up the charge and support your inner circle while growing your business at the same time.

Make It Happen!

—Jake & Gino

CHAPTER 1

What Comes First? The Money or the Deal?

When most investors contemplate entering the multifamily space, their biggest objection is "I don't have the money to take down my first deal." We've heard many new investors say, "Multifamily is a pie in the sky." Many of them have never heard of raising capital and creating a syndication (a way for investors to pool their capital together to acquire real estate), so they give up before they even start.

Mark Twain famously said, *"It ain't what you* don›t *know that gets you* into trouble. It›s what *you know* for sure that just *ain't* so." He was onto something. It's all too easy for limiting beliefs to hold people back from even trying.

When Jake and I began our investing journey, we didn't even consider raising capital to buy our first few deals. Our limiting beliefs kept us from thinking of friends and family. In fact, our first thousand units were purchased amongst three partners without raising any capital. We were able to buy these assets, increase the value of the deals, refinance out proceeds, and roll the proceeds into our next deals.

Eventually, we realized we would be able to target much larger acquisitions and create another stream of revenue using syndication, and that's when *Rand Partners* was born. By that point, we had an advantage. Our investor list had grown to over three hundred investors. We had a solid brand online, and our in-person events generated a ton of new interest from investors.

You may not have the experience we did, so where do you start? Do you go out and look for deals, and then hope to attract the money? Or do you build your list of investors and then go and hunt for deals? The simple answer is BOTH.

When we began our journey, we had no intention of raising capital, so our sole focus was on hunting for deals. It never hurts to hunt for deals, but you don't want to miss out on raising capital by creating pre-existing or substantive relationships with investors.

Now would be a good time to consider scheduling a call with a syndication attorney to discuss the type of offering you are going to create and how you are going to structure a syndication. This call will help you gain clarity on the rules and regulations of a syndication. For our first syndication, we spent over two hours on an initial consultation with our attorney discussing all of these topics. (Visit the Frequently

Asked Questions chapter at the end of the book for helpful definitions.)

Most new syndicators select Rule 506(b) of Regulation D because it allows the syndicator to raise capital from sophisticated investors (opposed to accredited investors). In your first deal, you go to people you trust—your friends and family. There are a couple of drawbacks with using the 506(b). First, there is no advertising or general solicitation allowed. No screaming from rooftops. No ads on social media that you found a deal. Second, you need to have a pre-existing relationship with each investor. That means if you find a deal right now, you can't raise capital from someone with whom you do not have a pre-existing relationship.

If you have a rich uncle or a Rolodex of wealthy accredited investors, the Rule 506(c) may be the way to go. Advertising is allowed, but you can only raise money from accredited investors. When you first start out, investors will normally want to see a track record, so just because you may have the relationships with the capital does not mean that they will invest in the deal. That's why the vast majority of new investors choose the 506(b) when starting out.

Again, if you are going to syndicate a deal using the Rule 506(b), you need the relationships first. So, begin creating pre-existing relationships with investors as you go out and underwrite deals. I've heard many gurus say that if you find the deal, the money will follow. If you don't have those pre-existing relationships, it doesn't matter if the money shows up. You've lost an opportunity to build your wealth.

When Jake and I had those three hundred investors on the list, we began to create the pre-existing relationship with each and every one of them. The rules are complex, which is why your syndication attorney is critical to your success. First, investors need to have certain financial qualifications. There also needs to be an undefined passage of time from when you met the investor and made them the offer. So, if you meet them on Monday, and you offer them the deal on Tuesday, you are violating the rule, according to the SEC.

When we meet a potential investor, we send them an email, get on a call with them to find out their investing goals and if they are compatible with ours, get to know their personal and professional life, and continue to reach out to them to grow the relationship. We use a CRM (Customer Relationship Management) to document and record all of these touch points.

You want to record all communication you have with your investors as well. The goal is to raise capital from investors who share the same goals and visions as you do, so it is imperative to find out more about them and their lives. Spend time on the front end selecting the right investors for your deal.

Take a few minutes now to create your power base—a list of friends, family, and co-workers to reach out to once you finish reading this book. Start reaching out to these acquaintances on LinkedIn or other social media platforms. You will be amazed how many people you know once you sit down and create your list. Now that you know how to overcome one of the most common barriers to multifamily, it's time to learn how to build these relationships by telling your own personal story.

CHAPTER 2
Creating Your Story

To raise capital, the first step is to educate yourself on the syndication model and know how you will start building your syndication. Once you've gone through this process, it's time to create your own personal story.

Remember that one of the main questions your investors will have is *Can I trust you?* By telling a true and compelling story about your journey to multifamily investing, you will build that trust.

Let's begin with the four components of a good story:

1. Identifiable characters
2. Authentic Emotion
3. Significant moment
4. Specific details

Using these four components, you can paint a vivid picture in the investor's mind—one they'll remember. You are the main character in the story, and you have to tell potential investors what attracted you to multifamily real estate and why you think it is the best investing vehicle out there. We like to share our AHA moment of why we selected multifamily, and express our emotions when we tell the story.

In your story, include specific details, such as dates, locations, and events that occurred. These specific details will paint the picture and elicit an emotional response from your investor.

It's not what you say. It's how you make them feel.

To give an example, let me share the story of how Jake and I met and why we chose multifamily real estate. This is our founder's story.

The year was 2009. I was in the kitchen sprinkling cayenne pepper on chicken breast and throwing the chicken onto a hot grill, while sautéing zucchini, peppers, mushrooms, and broccoli in garlic and oil. I owned Gino's Trattoria in New York, and ironically enough we called this dish Jake's Chicken.

I was cooking this dish for a catering that we were going to send to a doctor's office for a pharmaceutical rep named Jake Stenziano. Jake was good friends with my brother, but I had yet to meet him. All I knew was that Jake was an extremely focused, prepared young pharma rep who used our restaurant for many of his doctor's visits.

As I sweat over the hot grill, in walked Jake, all dressed up in a suit and tie. We instantly hit it off, and the conversation eventually trailed off to real estate. My brother Mark had introduced us because Jake had developed an intense interest in real estate from one of his doctor friends named Dr. Nescheiwat. Dr. Neshi, as Jake affectionately called him, was one of the last doctors who resisted selling his practice to one of the major medical groups in the area. How was he able to keep practicing medicine as he wished and maintain his autonomy? He credited real estate with giving him that freedom. Needless to say, Jake was intrigued by his success, and he wanted to learn more about how real estate could create the same success for him. I was also seeking to create more income with multifamily. I planned to eventually leave the restaurant and transition into multifamily full-time.

We continued the conversation over the next several months. During that time, Jake was feeling the pressure from the constant threat of layoffs, and my situation at the restaurant was deteriorating. I didn't understand how I could be working harder and getting paid less. We were both caught in the proverbial rat race.

Next thing I knew Jake was packing his bags and heading to Knoxville, Tennessee for no state income tax and a lower cost and better quality of living than New York. I didn't even know where that was, so I whipped out my laptop and logged into LoopNet, an online commercial real estate marketplace. To my astonishment, there were deals that actually cash flowed! I could hardly contain my excitement, and I told Jake to call me as soon as he got settled in his new apartment. Now that he lived there, he could visit these properties, and I could mentor him on all I knew about real estate investing.

After a couple weeks, Jake gave me a call. He shared how he moved to Knoxville by himself and is starting to feel homesick. Even though he wasn't sure about the decision, we began to look at deals and call real estate brokers to start scheduling some showings.

At first, we encountered a bit of success. But that success was short-lived. We started to get pushback from brokers for lack of credibility, and one even threatened us by saying, "Y'all ain't ever gonna do business down here!"

It was discouraging, but we were undeterred because of our situation. No one else knew we both had a huge WHY for succeeding in real estate, and a few bad encounters were not going to stop us. I was sick of working on the weekends and holidays, and Jake was sick of waiting by the phone to see if he was laid off from his job.

The next eighteen months proved challenging, but finally a broker sent us a twenty five-unit deal that made sense. We finally agreed on a price, and two months later we were proud owners of our first multifamily property. That was the beginning of an amazing partnership.

That first deal not only put us on the path to becoming multifamily entrepreneurs; it also introduced us to our broker Ricky G. Rick. We followed up that first deal with our second deal, only three months later—a thirty-six unit in need of some tender loving care. Talk about momentum. Six months later, Rick came through again with a one hundred and thirty-six unit deal, bringing our total units to one hundred and ninety seven.

*Thank God we embodied our motto: **Education x Action = Results®**.*

As we continued to grow our portfolio, we continued to educate ourselves through coaching and mentorship. Our success with mentors inspired us to create the Jake & Gino community to help others become successful multifamily investors. To this day, our goal is to provide education to those who want to exit the rat race and take back control of their finances and their time.

Now it's time to create your story. Make sure your story includes your WHY for multifamily investing. Finally, be sure to link your story to how you can help your potential investors. In the next chapter, we'll review the benefits of multifamily, but for now focus on your story. Take it from us: your story is worth a lot more than you think.

_____

_____

_____

_____

_____

_____

_____

_____

_____

_____

_____

_____

_____

_____

_____

_____

_____

_____

_____

_____

CHAPTER 3

Why Multifamily?

Multifamily has a multitude of benefits, and you want to convey these benefits in an easy to understand manner to your investors, without leaving them confused and overwhelmed. By doing so, you address the investor's question: *Can you help me?* Your story was a starting point, but now you're clearly outlining why multifamily is a great choice for them.

In your initial conversation, you should assume they know nothing about the multifamily sector. You are here to explain all the benefits to them. Here they are:

1. *Basic Human Need*

2. *Demographic Shift*

3. *Cash Flow*

4. *Hedge Against Inflation*

5. *Scalability*

6. *Tax Benefits*

In order to successfully pitch the idea, you don't want to start by explaining the features and benefits. Instead, start with your story and then ease into the benefits. If you jump into preferred rates of return and IRR, then your friend or family member will just tune you out. They'll become overwhelmed with all of the new jargon. You need to keep your listener engaged. So, start with your story, and then follow these steps to keep things interesting.

1. *Basic Human Need*: We like to give an overview of what multifamily is (providing housing for individuals) and then grab our potential investor's attention by saying:

Multifamily is a basic human need: Food, clothing, and apartments.

And the demand has been unaffected by the Internet!

Once you have their attention, you can dive into the demand for renting and how the demand has been unaffected by the Internet, whereas other asset classes, such as office and retail, have seen a huge shift in demand because of the Internet. Amazon is redefining the retail sector, causing many retailers to either downsize or focus on selling online. Video conferencing allows employees to work remotely, and many employers have downsized office space.

2. *Demographic Shift*: Recently, we recorded a podcast with Chris Porter, the author of *Big Shifts Ahead*. In his book, Chris dives into the demographics of the country and makes a compelling case of why we are becoming a renter nation. Listen to the podcast (see resources at the end of the book) to get a better understanding of these demographic shifts so you can explain them to your investor. In short, the shift is a huge benefit to any multifamily investor because the demand in only increasing for their product.

3. *Cash Flow*: We've all witnessed the roller coaster stock market, and how 401ks become 201ks. Multifamily, on the other hand, is a stable, hard asset that produces a monthly yield, AKA cash flow. You can compare it to a stock that produces a quarterly dividend. You are not only speculating that the price will rise; you are blending capital appreciation with cash flow. At this point, you can also remind the investor that multifamily is a basic human need.

If it don't cash flow, then let the grass grow!

4. *Hedge Against Inflation*: You want to make sure to explain this concept in layman's terms. Inflation is the increase in the supply of money, and the end result is the increase in prices. Explain to your investor that the government loves to print money, and there seems to be no end in sight for the printing presses to shut down.

Then explain that inflation leads to two positive results for multifamily: Rents will rise, and the value of the asset over time will also rise. Baby boomers who bought a home back in the 70s and 80s understand this principle well. Their homes appreciated in value because of inflation. Over time, investors view holding hard assets as more favorable due to inflation and the erosion of the value of fiat currency. Fiat currency is a government issued currency, such as the U.S. dollar, and has no intrinsic value. Here, you can drive this point home by telling them that a cup of coffee back in 1970 cost $.25, and now we pay three bucks for that same cup of java!

Apartment owners grow rich in their sleep

5. *Scalability*: This concept may be a bit more difficult to explain to a newer investor. So keep things simple. Explain that investing in multifamily benefits from the economies of scale and the fact that all of the units are contiguous (located in the same area). Let them know that it is much easier to manage a twenty five-unit apartment complex than to manage twenty-five single-family homes scattered throughout the city. The costs are much lower to run a multifamily, and it is much easier to grow or scale the business.

6. *Tax Benefits*: Cost segregation is *a commonly used strategic tax planning tool that allows companies and individuals who have constructed, purchased, expanded, or remodeled any kind of real estate* to increase cash flow by accelerating depreciation deductions and deferring federal and state income taxes. (Thanks to KBKG for that concise definition). What does that mean to a neophyte? You get to keep more of your income because you are able to utilize the depreciation, a non-cash expense, as a write off against your income.

It's not what you make. It's what you keep!

To run a cost segregation study, you need a team of engineers to determine the useful life of various components of the apartment. For example, the doors of the apartment may only have a five-year timeline, so you can depreciate their value on a faster schedule. This breaks up the total value of the apartment into either five, seven, fifteen, or 27.5 years, allowing you to depreciate much more each year.

Currently, the government is also incentivizing apartment owners with bonus depreciation, allowing all of the five, seven, and fifteen-year schedules to be depreciated 100% in year 1! This alone has attracted many high net worth investors to multifamily. The bottom line is: less tax and more after-tax income. It is music to a doctor or lawyer's ears when they hear tax benefits, so be sure to include it when you speak to an investor. (Visit the resource section for a video on cost segregation.)

As you discuss all these benefits, remember not to overwhelm your friends and family with details. Simply be prepared to mention each benefit and answer any questions the investor has. Whenever possible, link your story to the benefits, explaining what drew you to multifamily in the first place.

Once you've explained all the benefits, there's one more topic to discuss. Ask the investor if they have any funds in an IRA or a retirement account, and then ask them, "Have you ever considered investing a part of your retirement account into real estate?" I can almost guarantee you will get a blank stare. Most people have no idea that is an option.

Mention to them the Self Directed IRA, an individual retirement account, which allows individuals to invest in alternative investments. There is a massive opportunity to raise capital from the retirement accounts, because ONLY 4% of the total money held in retirement accounts are held in Self Directed IRAs. Most investors don't even know they exist. It is much easier to raise capital from a retirement account because investors' money is locked away for years before they will be able to access it without incurring exorbitant fees. On our last capital raise, around 50% of the capital came from investors' retirement accounts.

Now that you've shared your story with the investor, and discussed the benefits of investing in multifamily, it's time to show your investors how it all works.

CHAPTER 4

How Does It Work?

By providing investors with the ins and outs of multi-family—in a way that's easy to understand—you answer their final question: *Do you care about me?* As you follow our advice here, consider your listener's perspective. They need to feel you truly care that they win. Otherwise, they'll lose their trust and won't feel you can truly help them.

We've found that using stories and pictures are the two best ways to convey what investing in a multifamily looks like. We use this visual with investors for them to get an idea of the process of investing in a multifamily deal.

By sharing stories and showing this image, your investors should understand what you look for when investing in a multifamily:

- Population growth

- Employment growth

- High % of rent to own (larger base of customers)

- Diverse employment sectors

- Positive net migration

Explain to your potential investor that you look for these characteristics because they all lead to a positive market to invest in, where it will be easier to attract tenants, and where you will be able to maintain and even increase rents.

Once your investors understand why you are investing in a market, you should move into a conversation about how you make money in multifamily. Here, you can make the comparisons between owning one home versus an apartment complex consisting of multiple units.

Begin by asking the investor what happens if the single family home becomes vacant. Who is going to pay the mortgage? You are! In an apartment complex, on the other hand, even if you lose one or two tenants you still have enough tenants to cover the mortgage.

It's also important to explain how you have control when affecting the value of multifamily. In single-family homes, valuation is derived from the sales comparison approach— comparing one property to comparable or recently sold properties in the market. You are beholden to the forces of the market, and if the market decides to decline there isn't much you can do, other than watch your equity evaporate. Couple that with poor cash flow from a single-family home, and your investor will start to realize why you have chosen multifamily.

The value of a multifamily property is determined by this formula: *Net Operating Income (NOI) divided by the Cap Rate.* NOI is calculated as net revenue minus operating expenses. The market determines the Cap Rate. Therefore, the way you can control and increase the value of a property is through increasing the NOI. When you can increase annual NOI, you not only increase cash flows but are directly impacting the value of the property. For every dollar you increase the income on each unit, the property goes up in value, resulting in a multiplier effect.

There are two ways to increase the NOI: to increase income and to decrease expenses. We let our investors know that we target the Mom and Pop apartment owners because these owners typically have much higher expenses due to lack of systems and inefficiencies. How can you have your investors spot a Mom and Pop? Tell them to be on the lookout the next time they drive to work or the supermarket for any apartments that have unkempt landscaping, gutters hanging off, or any other form of deferred maintenance. These owners tend to be motivated and often do not know the true value of their property. Explain that these are the owners you buy from.

You can also discuss how you increase the income on a property by increasing rents and increasing ancillary streams of revenue. Share how you focus on ancillary revenue, such as laundry income, move in fees, pet fees, storage fees, parking fees, and billing back utilities to the residents. The goal is to paint the picture to your investors that multifamily is a business where you have multiple levers to create value on the property, and you are not constrained by market forces to create value.

*The average millionaire has seven streams of income.
How many do you have?*

Once you purchase a multifamily, investors get paid in two
ways: They receive distributions from collected cash flows
throughout the holding period, in addition to equity gains
upon sale/refinance. You want to discuss equity splits with
your investor and preferred rates of return, but don't do this
until they understand the vehicle of multifamily and are
convinced that it will achieve their goals. If they are not yet
convinced, they will begin to tune you out.

I recommend listening to Oren Klaff's podcasts (see the
resource section). He does a masterful job in what he calls
inception—embedding an idea in someone's mind so they think
it's their own. Oren shows that in today's world, products are
bought, not sold. Because of the Internet, people's skepticism
is at an all time high, so you need to be masterful in your
approach. Your investors should think the idea of investing
in multifamily was their own by the time they finish talking
with you.

Once inception has set in and you have convinced your
investor, discuss with them the fun part: how they get paid.
You can share with them your business plan, preferred rate of
return, and equity splits with investors.

As one final note, be sure you fully understand Internal Rate of Return (IRR), a metric that calculates the average annual return your investors can expect to realize from their investment. The IRR is the percentage of interest you earn on each dollar you invest in a deal over the entire holding period. Learn how to calculate IRR so you can discuss it with your investors.

You are now equipped to begin offering the opportunity to your friends and family and start growing your syndication business. Start by developing relationships with potential investors. As you move into conversations about multifamily investing, remember to start with your story, then explain the benefits, and finally provide insight into how it all works. And remember to have fun along the way. Here's one final Jake & Gino ism to bring into your next conversation:

> *Let your job pay for your apartments and your apartments pay for your lifestyle.*

Keep the *Multifamily Real Estate Booklet* handy, and never be afraid to offer others the opportunity to join your team.

MIH!

Jake & Gino

CHAPTER 5

Frequently Asked Questions

Here, we've laid out all potential questions that your friends and family might have. It is imperative that you are prepared for all of these questions.

Note: We have answered these questions as if we were speaking to our investors. Please customize the answers to you.

1. What is syndication?

Syndication is the pooling of capital from investors to participate towards a common goal in an investment. The general partner (the partner who puts the deal together and implements the business plan) builds this syndication with limited partners (passive investors).

2. How do I get started investing with you?

You can get started investing once you have registered for our investor portal and have had an introduction phone call with someone from our team. To register for our investor portal, click here: Jake & Gino.

From here, you will begin receiving monthly newsletters and deal announcements that will explain what you need to do in order to partner with us on each specific deal.

3. What type of accounts can I use to invest with?

We currently support personal investment accounts, joint accounts, and certain entity accounts (Trusts, Limited Liability Companies, Limited Partnerships, C Corporations, and S Corporations). You will need to contact your IRA, QRP, and 401k provider to obtain the required forms if investing with a retirement account. Returns will be issued to the retirement account. Talk with your CPA and retirement plan custodian to learn more about the tax treatment.

4. How are payments to investors determined and how often do they occur?

Distributions are a function of income generation at a property for a given period. We generally target distributing the offered preferred return each quarter, in addition to any additional upside at the end of Q4 each year. If a property performance is strong, distribution levels can be above projections, and if property performance is weaker than expected, distributions may be below targets.

5. How will you communicate with the investor?

We hold quarterly webinar updates with our investors, send out monthly newsletters, and send out a K-1 statement from us for your tax filings each March. We are also available any time to jump on a call to answer any questions.

6. If I need money for an emergency, is there an option to exit the investment early?

Our investments should be considered illiquid, but we will make our best effort to accommodate emergencies/unusual circumstances in which we will either find another investor to purchase your existing position or buy it out ourselves.

7. What is an accredited investor?

The SEC defines an accredited investor as an individual with a net worth of at least $1 million, or an annual income of $200,000 for someone filing single, or $300,000 for those filing as joint income with a spouse, for at least three years. An individual and one filing jointly needs their net worth to exceed $1 million at the time of the purchase, excluding the value of the person's primary residence.

8. What is a sophisticated investor?

The SEC defines a sophisticated investor as an individual who has enough knowledge and experience in business matters to evaluate the risks and merits of an investment. In syndications, which are offered through the 506(b) exemption, sophisticated, non-accredited investors are permitted to invest as long as they have a preexisting relationship with the sponsor.

9. What is the hold period?

We typically underwrite for a five to seven year hold period, depending on the performance of the asset and market conditions.

10. What is the Internal Rate of Return of the investment?

As of today's market conditions, we are underwriting for an 8-10% cash on cash return, with an IRR in the range of 15-20%. You may also see 2x multiple, which means if you invest $50,000 into the deal, the target is a double, or grow your money to $100,000 in five years through distributions and profit at sale.

11. What fees are involved in an investment?

We charge an acquisition fee of 3% based on the purchase price for sourcing, putting the deal together, and running the deal. We also charge an asset management fee of 1% of total capital raised every year to manage the asset.

12. Are you investing in the deal with your own capital?

We typically invest between 10-20% of the capital needed for each project.

13. What is the minimum investment?

Our typical minimum investment is $50,000.

14. Can I invest through an LLC?

Yes, you can invest with an LLC.

15. What is Rule 506(b)?

Rule 506(b) eliminates the need for people issuing securities to register if they meet certain qualifications. Investors can raise an unlimited amount of money from accredited investors and up to thirty-five non-accredited investors. No general solicitation or advertising is allowed for the investment.

16. What is Rule 506(c)?

Rule 506(c) allows for general solicitation of the investment if all of the investors in the offering are accredited and the company takes reasonable steps to verify that they are accredited.

17. What is a General Partner?

A General Partner (GP) is an investor who takes active involvement and assumes a day-to-day role in managing the investment. He or she is responsible for any debts incurred with investment.

18. What is a Limited Partner?

A Limited Partner (LP) is a passive investor in the deal. They have limited liability in the deal, and their risk is limited to the amount of capital they invest. They are not signers on the loan, and bear no responsibility for the performance of the deal.

19. What does the timeline/process look like?

Once we have a property under contract, the due diligence takes around 60 days to perform. We begin the equity raise process with investors, which takes approximately four weeks. We send out marketing materials to all investors and hold a webinar to discuss the opportunity. Investors then have the chance to reserve a spot, review the Private Placement Memorandum, and sign. We work on a first come, first serve basis, so time is of the essence to reserve a spot. About 2-3 weeks later, we close on the property. Approximately 60 days later, the first investor distribution will occur.

20. What is a Private Placement Memorandum?

The PPM is a legal document given to all prospective investors in a real estate investment. It is designed to provide potential investors with full disclosure based on the requirements of the federal securities law. It states the objectives, risks, and terms of the investment.

21. What is a subscription agreement?

According to investopedia.com, a subscription agreement is an investor's application to join a limited partnership. It is also a two-way guarantee between a company and a subscriber. The company agrees to sell a certain number of shares at a specific price, and in return the subscriber promises to buy the shares at the predetermined price.

RECOMMENDED READS:

Wheelbarrow Profits by Jake & Gino

The Richest Man in Babylon by George S. Clason

The Honey Bee by Jake & Gino

Think & Grow Rich by Napoleon Hill

Rich Dad Poor Dad by Robert Kiyosaki

Killing Sacred Cows by Garrett Gunderson

Principles of Real Estate Syndication by Samuel Freshman

How To Legally Raise Private Money by Kim Lisa Taylor

RECOMMENDED PODCASTS

- Visit the Jake & Gino Channel on iTunes to listen to these podcasts.

- Unlocking Investors with Oren Klaff

- Making It Stick with Oren Klaff

- Negotiate Like An FBI Hostage Negotiator with Chris Voss

- How To Raise Money Using Your SDIRA with Scott Maurer

- Chris Porter & Big Shifts Ahead

- Negotiating The Waters Of Syndication with Kim Lisa Taylor

- Cost Segregation For Dummies with Tom Wheelwright

- Stop Giving Your Money Away with Tom Wheelwright

- Active or Passive Investing with Jake & Gino